SCOTTISH CITYLINK COACHES

DAVID DEVOY

AMBERLEY

First published 2019

Amberley Publishing
The Hill, Stroud
Gloucestershire, GL5 4EP

www.amberley-books.com

Copyright © David Devoy, 2019

The right of David Devoy to be identified as the Author of this work has been asserted in accordance with the Copyrights, Designs and Patents Act 1988.

ISBN 978 1 4456 9147 3 (print)
ISBN 978 1 4456 9148 0 (ebook)

All rights reserved. No part of this book may be reprinted or reproduced or utilised in any form or by any electronic, mechanical or other means, now known or hereafter invented, including photocopying and recording, or in any information storage or retrieval system, without the permission in writing from the Publishers.

British Library Cataloguing in Publication Data.
A catalogue record for this book is available from the British Library.

Typesetting by Aura Technology and Software Services, India. Printed in the UK.

Introduction

Perhaps the delivery of the prototype MCW Metroliner TSX 1Y to the Scottish Bus Group in 1983 gave us a clue as to the then current thinking regarding the group's express services. It was delivered in a livery of yellow with blue stripes, unlike any of the existing colour schemes then in use. The repainting of Eastern Scottish Leyland Tiger TFS 321Y into a similar scheme with Scottish Cityliner names gave a second clue. The Scottish Cityliner name began to appear on other group coaches, but generally was white and grey with a strip of each company's traditional colour added. There is no doubt that the coaches introduced by many of the independents left the group far behind. Forward orders placed began to include small batches of higher spec coaches. Scottish Citylink was launched on 1 October 1983, but excluded the London services at this stage. Twenty-three services were initially brought together under the Citylink banner, with more added as time went by. Seventy new coaches were to be liveried for the new services, with some older vehicles upgraded to a similar spec. The budget was around £6.5 million, and TV and press advertising was used to promote the new era.

Star of the 1983 Scottish Motor Show staged at the Kelvin Hall in Glasgow was an Alexander TC type-bodied Leyland Tiger for Midland Scottish. This carried Citylink livery and featured bonded glazing, stretched side panels, a plug door, soft trim and 'Diplomat' seats. New coaches began to appear with various group subsidiaries in Citylink livery during 1984. Forward orders for 1985 included a further seventy-five coaches for Citylink and the London fleets. Over seventy services were now running under the Citylink branding, including some summer-only departures. A small fleet of double-deck coaches was also beginning to arrive, for use on shorter routes. Some journeys were also being upgraded to 'Cordon Bleu' status, and featured drinks vending machines. Towards the end of the year it was announced that the Bus Group was to be reformed to produce eleven operating companies.

A new company, to be headed by Alan Wilson, was to be set up in March 1985 to plan and market Citylink and London services, as well as managing Buchanan bus station in Glasgow, St Andrew Square bus station in Edinburgh and the Bus Group office in London. The name chosen was Scottish Citylink Coaches Ltd, although it was not envisaged that the company would own any vehicles at that time and would hire in suitably liveried coaches as required.

The Bus Group acquired a major competitor when Newton's of Dingwall sold out at the end of 1985. The company had built up a jointly operated network of services in the far north with Allander Travel of Milngavie. Citylink took over the operation of services linking Glasgow and Edinburgh to Scrabster, Thurso and Inverness. The London services were brought under the Citylink umbrella for marketing purposes. Coach tours previously operated by Midland

Bluebird and Eastern Scottish were to be operated by Scottish Citylink under the Clansman Scottish name from 1986 onwards.

January 1986 saw Allander Travel cancel its Glasgow to Inverness services, but it was given some regular workings on the Glasgow to Edinburgh Citylink service by way of compensation. Under new legislation introduced in 1986 Scottish Citylink Coaches had to apply for an operator licence to register all the services in its own name. Up until this point they had been registered under Kelvin Scottish for convenience. A further side effect of this meant that the company had to own at least one vehicle of its own and Western B924 CGA was duly re-registered under Citylink. The legal address was Buchanan bus station, Killermont Street, Glasgow. As the Scottish Bus Group prepared for privatisation, Citylink franchises were no longer exclusive to the SBG subsidiaries. Private companies such as Clan Coaches of Kyle, Crawford Coaches of Neilston, Dodd's of Troon, Park's of Hamilton, Rapson's Coaches of Inverness and West Coast Motors of Campbeltown were awarded Citylink contracts and provided vehicles of their own for this work in Citylink livery. Good publicity was achieved with the sponsoring of the Glasgow Marathon, including the provision of coaches throughout the event.

The decision to limit the use of the Citylink brand to long-distance and inter-city services was taken in January 1987; consequently many local commuter routes to the south-west of Glasgow were taken under the Clydeside Quicksilver brand. Meanwhile, more routes were upgraded to 'Cordon Bleu' standards. A new service was introduced between Glasgow and Gatwick Airport on behalf of Ashtak Travel Ltd. In the summer of 1988 services between Glasgow and Skye were disrupted after the ferry operator CalMac imposed a huge fare increase for coaches using its service linking Kyle of Lochalsh and Kyleakin. Scottish Citylink flatly refused to pay the higher charges, and passengers had to change coaches on either side of the water. Thankfully, common sense prevailed and an agreement was reached later in the year. The joint agreements between National Express and Scottish Citylink were terminated at the end of 1989 after the Office of Fair Trading indicated that it was not happy with the status quo. Both companies stated that they would both operate the same levels of service independently of each other. Citylink declared that it would help it to expand beyond its artificially constrained market into the rest of the UK and Europe. Bruce of Airdrie launched its Londonliner service in competition with Citylink. In return Citylink retaliated with Red Knight coaches, with a similar range of places served. It must have worked as Citylink took over the running of the Londonliner service, with Bruce sub-contracted to run it. A joint service linking Inverness and Skye was launched in conjunction with Clan Garage, while Rapson's of Alness also joined the network.

National Express set up a Scottish subsidiary based on the former Stagecoach of Perth express coach business and began to compete more vigorously, while upgrading more routes to Rapide spec. Meanwhile, Citylink was busy recruiting non-Bus Group partners throughout the UK to strengthen its network. Work for thirty-three coaches was shared between Bruce, Rapson's, Gold Circle of Airdrie, Crawford's of Neilston, Silver Fox of Renfrew, Dodd's of Troon, West Coast Motors, Skyeways, Chesterfield Transport, West Midlands Travel and MacPherson of Burton-on-Trent. Extra competition was experienced when Green's of Kirkintilloch and Silver Coach Lines of Edinburgh challenged Citylink on the Glasgow to Edinburgh corridor. The state-owned Scottish Bus Group announced that it was to be privatised. Citylink was included, but both Buchanan and St Andrew Square bus stations were to be excluded. Another side effect of the forthcoming privatisation was that the Scottish Bus Group operators were not investing in their fleets and were beginning to look poor against the coaches being provided by the independent operators. Rival National Express claimed that it had obtained 50 per cent of the Scotland–London market, 80 per cent of the Scotland–rest of England market and 35 per cent of the internal Scottish market, so Citylink clearly needed to respond quickly.

The company was offered for sale in May 1990. Kelvin Central Buses withdrew from all Citylink work and Northern Scottish withdrew from cross-border services. Ulsterbus became a partner in a new Stranraer to London facility along with Dodd's of Troon and Western Scottish. Many services were reduced or withdrawn between Scotland and some English regions after strong competition with National Express, although other routes were strengthened. In August 1990 'preferred bidder' status was granted to the management and employees of Citylink regarding the purchase of the company. Other bidders were Park's of Hamilton, National Express and a joint venture between West Coast Motors and Skyeways.

A new holding company was formed to take over Scottish Citylink from the end of August, known as Clansman Travel & Leisure Ltd. The company was sold for £265,000 and needed around 120 coaches to run the network. A revised livery was introduced in early 1991 to refresh the brand, designed by Ray Stenning. Included was the slogan, 'Citylinking…smart thinking'. In a surprise move, Clansman Travel and Rapson's of Alness formed a joint company to acquire the business of Bruce of Airdrie. Contracts with former and current SBG companies were being renegotiated in a bid to improve standards. Fairline Coaches of Glasgow was contracted to operate the Glasgow Airport shuttle with four new minibuses. Most of the company's Clansman Monarch Coach Holidays work was operated by Park's of Hamilton, and thirteen vehicles were used on these workings. A new challenger appeared in November 1991 when Knightrider Travel began low-cost services from both Glasgow and Edinburgh to London. Citylink responded by reintroducing Bruce's Londonliner low-cost service, which covered an identical route. Highland Bus & Coach became jointly owned by Clansman Travel and Rapson's of Alness, and would provide three coaches for the network.

The year 1992 saw Clansman Travel & Leisure renamed as Saltire Holdings, with its headquarters moved from Glasgow to Edinburgh. Other interests included a catering business, a chain of newsagents in Glasgow and shares in a London-based air travel firm in partnership with a French company. Eighty-two coaches were required to operate the winter schedules.

May 1993 saw the ownership of Saltire Holdings pass to National Express Group PLC in a £5.1 million deal. As part of the deal it was announced that National Express was to sell off its Perth-based subsidiary to British Bus. Saltire would also sell off its Bruce's Coaches company. The sale of these two companies realised £1.2 million. Rapson's took full control of Highland Bus & Coach. British Bus closed the Bruce's Coaches operation only two weeks after it purchased it after a substantial amount of Citylink work was lost. The Office of Fair Trading decided to investigate the National Express takeover of Saltire Holdings. Cross-border services to England were replaced by National Express services, leaving Citylink with Scottish domestic services, and coordinated timetabling and ticketing was introduced between the two operators. Express Travel of Perth closed down in August 1994 after failure to agree rates for coach contracts with National Express. The Glasgow Airport service operated by Fairline was terminated, but it registered its own service against Citylink.

October 1995 saw Rapson's split its Highland fleet into two separate companies following the setting up of Highland Country. On 1 January 1996 National Express purchased the business of Gaelicbus of Ballachulish through its Scottish Citylink subsidiary. Purchased around the same time was Highland Country from Rapson's Coaches, with Martin's of Spean Bridge adding a further two coaches. A 25 per cent shareholding was also taken in West Coast Motors of Campbeltown. The Glasgow–Edinburgh service was upgraded to a coach every fifteen minutes. In September Citylink purchased a 25 per cent stake in Clan Garage (Kyle), better known as Skyeways Coaches.

A significant event occurred in May 1997, when National Express won the seven-year franchise to operate Scotrail, owner of Scotland's railways. The Monopolies and Mergers Commission ruled this would give National Express a monopoly on long-distance services in Scotland and ordered National Express to sell Scottish Citylink Coaches in December 1997 or face a referral to the Commission. The company was given a six-month window to sell Scottish Citylink. It had made £1 million profit for the year, so would be sought after.

In March 1998 a new style of Scottish Citylink fleet name began to appear on the coaches. In April it was announced that as Citylink Coaches shared its management with Highland Country, both companies were up for sale. The Department for Trade and Industry set the date for the divestment of Citylink as 16 June. Over a dozen potential purchasers expressed an interest. In August 1998 Scottish Citylink was sold to Metroline, a London-based company, for a sum of £10.3 million, while Highland Country was bought back by Rapson's Coaches for £4 million.

Skyeways and Citylink parted company in October 1999 after falling out over contracts, so Park's of Hamilton and Rapson's Coaches began operating the services from Portree to both Inverness and Glasgow. Skyeways launched competing services in December.

In February 2000 Metroline, owner of Citylink, agreed to a £73.8 million takeover by Singapore Group DelGro, and became the first UK stock market-listed bus group to fall into foreign hands. The livery was updated and refreshed once again in early 2001, with less emphasis on the Scottish part of the fleet name. October saw Park's of Hamilton begin operating journeys for Stagecoach Glasgow on the Scottish Citylink Glasgow/East Kilbride to Edinburgh routes under a franchise agreement. The following year Arriva Scotland West rebranded the buses used on the Glasgow to Glasgow Airport route operated jointly with Fairline Coaches of Glasgow into Scottish Citylink colours. The shares held by Citylink in West Coast Motors were repurchased by the Craig family on 17 July 2002. The company was named as the official shuttle bus provider for the T in the Park music festival. The company began trading in the Republic of Ireland, acquiring Cummer Commercials, which operated on the Dublin to Galway route (and traded as CityLink Express). The route was rebranded to the yellow-blue Citylink livery and expanded to provide services from Galway to Shannon.

The year 2003 saw improvements for passengers with new bus stations opening in both Edinburgh and Inverness. This was also backed up by a television and cinema advertising campaign and ten new coaches introduced onto Glasgow to Edinburgh service after a 20 per cent increase in loadings. Competition drastically increased after Stagecoach introduced its Megabus concept to Scotland from 8 September, with bookings made online at bargain fares when booked early. Services linked Glasgow and Edinburgh to Dundee. Meanwhile, the Firstbus service linking Edinburgh to Stirling University was taken over by Citylink from the end of August.

Stagecoach ramped up the competition in 2004 with the purchase of Motorvator, which was a joint venture between Bruce of Shotts and Long's of Salsburgh and linked Glasgow and Edinburgh. Citylink responded by removing Stagecoach from all Citylink work, replacing it with Park's vehicles. Stagecoach then upped the frequency of the Motorvator service and expanded the Megabus concept to include Aberdeen and Inverness.

In September 2005 ComfortDelGro and Stagecoach agreed to a joint venture to provide express coach services in Scotland, ending the competition between the two operators. Under the terms of the agreement, Stagecoach gained a 35 per cent shareholding in Scottish Citylink and in return granted certain rights to the Megabus and Motorvator brands in Scotland. Despite being the minority shareholder, Stagecoach appeared to assume operational control. Stagecoach staff replaced much of the former Citylink management, while Stagecoach's Scottish subsidiaries began operating many of the routes formerly operated by subcontractors displaced from Citylink work. Citylink service numbers, timetables and routes were also sacrificed in favour of Megabus where the two brands overlapped. The Office of Fair Trading took an interest after many of Citylink's established contractors lost their work on the network. The Competition Commission declared that it wanted the joint venture to sell some of its services on the 'Saltire Cross'. This meant the Glasgow–Aberdeen and Edinburgh–Inverness services, which all passed through Perth at the centre.

In 2007 Citylink relinquished services 901 and 906 in favour of McGill's of Greenock. These routes served Glasgow to Gourock and Largs. Stagecoach introduced 15-metre-long tri-axle coaches on some of the busier services. The company complied with the Competition Commission's ruling in early 2008 by selling a portion of the network to Park's of Hamilton. Park's began to add its own names in place of Citylink, but maintained a similar livery of blue and yellow. The new Park's workings were known as 'City to City', but could still be booked through the citylink.co.uk and megabus.com websites as well as the Park's site. In June 2008, West Coast Motors began to run its own services to Argyll after a disagreement with Citylink. The company had been operating these services for over twenty years under the Citylink brand. A compromise was reached in September and all competing services were withdrawn. West Coast was allowed to keep its traditional red and cream colours for coaches on these services.

In 2010, Citylink launched the 'Gold' brand for services between Glasgow and Aberdeen or Inverness. The Citylink Gold brand is similar to the Stagecoach Gold brand used by Stagecoach bus subsidiaries and offers a more luxurious service with leather seats, free Wi-Fi and extra services aboard. With Citylink Gold, passengers are offered free tea and coffee on the bus. Three services per day in each direction on routes from Glasgow to Aberdeen and Glasgow to Inverness are designated as Citylink Gold. Fares have remained the same with Super Singles available on the routes, as they were while under standard Citylink branding. In Ireland Callinan of Claregalway was contracted to operate all Citylink services in that country.

From 14 July 2014 the Glasgow–Fort William–Skye services passed to a new joint venture set up by West Coast Motors and Shiel Buses. Shiel Buses added a yellow Citylink rear onto its silver livery with appropriate lettering.

John Bruce launched an hourly rival CityXpress service linking Glasgow and Edinburgh after losing Citylink work in February 2015, with Citylink responding by adding route branding to its coaches and introducing low-fare deals. On 11 December 2015, a London St Pancras railway station to Stansted Airport service commenced under the Stansted Citylink banner. In January 2019, Betterez, a Toronto-based tech start-up specialising in modernising the ticketing and reservations systems of operators in the ground travel industry, announced that Scottish Citylink had selected it as its ticketing platform.

CSG 793S was a Seddon Pennine VII/Plaxton Supreme Express C45F purchased new by Eastern Scottish in April 1978, and refurbished to launch Scottish Citylink. It was captured in Glasgow's Anderston bus station while working on the Edinburgh Express service.

This was a Seddon Pennine VII/Alexander T Type C49F purchased new by Western SMT in September 1977. It was given Scottish Citylink livery to operate the former MacBraynes service to Tarbert and was based at Thornliebank depot in Glasgow. It was later re-registered as WLT 501.

BSG 544W was a Leyland Tiger TRCTL11/3R/Duple Dominant III C46Ft purchased new by Eastern Scottish as its XH544 in July 1981. This was the prototype for a new generation of coaches for the Scottish Bus Group for use on the prestigious Scotland to London route. It is shown later in life with Midland Scottish after a rebuild to allow larger windows to be fitted.

HSD 707N was a Volvo B58-61/Alexander M Type C42Ft purchased new by Western SMT as its V2536 in April 1975 for the London service. It was downgraded for use on shorter services worked under the Cityliner/Citylink banner, reseated to C45F and fitted with express doors. It was captured in Irvine working a limited stop Cityliner service to Troon and Ayr. On disposal it would join Hamilton's of Uxbridge for further service.

E161 YGB was a Leyland Lion LDTL11/1R/Alexander RH Type CH49/37F delivered to Clydeside Scottish as its number 161 in December 1987. It had originally been ordered by Kelvin Scottish and was intended to be registered as D853 RDS. It is shown in Glasgow working on a commuter service, but these were later rebranded under the Clydeside Quicksilver brand.

GGE 131X was a Volvo B10M-61/Duple Goldliner C46Ft purchased new by Western Scottish as its V131 in July 1982. It was originally used on the London service, but had been rebuilt and re-registered as GSU 950 when snapped. It would be rebodied by East Lancs as a service bus in February 1998.

A148 BSC was an MCW Metroliner DR130/4 CH69DT new to Eastern Scottish in April 1984 as its fleet number XCMM147. It was painted in Scottish Citylink livery and used on the London service when new, but was working on the Glasgow–Edinburgh route in this view taken in Waterloo Place in Edinburgh.

A167 UGB was a Leyland Tiger TRCLXC/2RH/Plaxton Paramount Express C49F delivered new to Western Scottish as its number L167 in April 1984. It was transferred to Clydeside Scottish just over one year later. It then moved to Midland Scottish as its MPT135, and was re-registered as TSV 730. It was burnt out in a fire at Oban depot and scrapped.

BMS 512Y is a Leyland Tiger TRBTL11/2R/Alexander TE Type C49F new to Midland in April 1983 and allocated to Perth depot. It would pass to Strathtay Scottish and later be re-registered as VLT 298. It went south to join the fleet of Wootens/Tiger Line and became BIG 4269 before returning home to John Carson's WJC fleet.

B175 FFS was a Volvo Citybus B10M-50/Alexander RVC CH70F new to Fife Scottish as its FRA75 in October 1984. It was foisted upon Western in 1987 to cover for two E registration Citybuses that Fife purloined, and on disposal passed to Cunninghame District Council for conversion into a playbus. That was all still a long way away, however, when FRA75 was leaving Dunfermline on its way to Perth.

A121 ESG was a Leyland Tiger TRCTL11/3RH/Duple Caribbean C47Ft delivered new as Midland MPT121 in June 1984. It was re-registered as SSU 821, and is shown arriving in Aberdeen on Citylink service 564. The Caribbean was built by Duple between 1983 and 1986, and replaced the high-floor Goldliner variant of the long-running Duple Dominant range as Duple's premium coach body of the mid-1980s.

MNS 9Y was a Leyland Tiger TRBTL11/2R/Alexander TE Type C49F purchased new by Central Scottish as its LT9 in April 1983, seen loading in Edinburgh. It tended to work on the Paisley–East Kilbride–Edinburgh corridor. Later in life it moved to Fife Scottish as its number 469.

A179 UGB was a Leyland Tiger TRCLXC/2RH/Plaxton Paramount Express C49F new as Western Scottish L179 in April 1984. It was running as a Clydeside Scottish vehicle on a Clansman Monarch tour. It would later be re-registered as 54 CLT before passing to Lough Swilly, where it became 84-DL-2122.

A128 ESG was a Leyland Tiger TRCTL11/3RH/Duple Laser C46Ft purchased new by Midland Scottish in April 1984 and captured as it leaves Stirling. It would pass to Kelvin Scottish as its 4232 in June 1985 and was later re-registered to WLT 676. It was running on the Glasgow to Aberdeen service.

D555 CJF was a Volvo B10M-61/Plaxton Paramount 3500 C53Ft purchased new by Macpherson of Coalville in May 1987 for use on Scottish Citylink work, and was caught leaving Glasgow en route to Aberdeen. Macpherson was established in 1986 as a family-owned business. Harry Macpherson had always wanted to drive buses as a child so on his first retirement in 1985 he made his dream come true and bought a coach business.

B337 RLS was a Leyland Tiger TRCTL11/2RH/Plaxton Paramount 3200 C49F new as Eastern Scottish YL 337 in April 1985. It was on a Clansman Monarch Tour and had stopped for a cuppa at Bridge of Orchy. It would later become WSV 137.

A331 BSC was a Leyland Tiger TRCTL11/2R/Plaxton Paramount Express C49F delivered new to Eastern Scottish as its fleet number CL331 in January 1984. It is shown in Glasgow while working on the Glasgow Airport to Edinburgh service. It would later be re-registered as A20 SMT, eventually joining the Lowland Scottish fleet.

One of the English independents engaged by Citylink to work cross-border services was McPherson of Coalville, whose DAF SB3000/Van Hool is seen in Glasgow. When National Express took over Citylink in 1993, Citylink's cross-border services ceased, with the exception of a few seasonal Blackpool services and the Stranraer to London, which remained Citylink for a while.

L300 WCM was a Volvo B10M-60/Jonckheere Deauville C53F purchased new by West Coast Motors in March 1994, seen nearing its terminus in Glasgow. West Coast has worked both with and against Citylink at various times, but a good working relationship has been built up over the years.

C672 KDS was a Volvo B10M-61/Caetano Algarve C49Ft purchased new by Park's of Hamilton in March 1986. It is shown in the ownership of Bruce of Airdrie while working on a tour for David Urquhart Travel. Bruce used many non-standard variations of the Scottish Citylink livery. The use of independents was a factor in raising standards on the network.

Scottish Citylink Coaches

GSG 134T was a Leyland Leopard PSU3E/4R/Duple Dominant C49F purchased new by Fife Scottish in November 1978. Fife was losing private hire work at an alarming rate to both Rennie's and Moffat & Williamson and this batch of coaches allowed the company to compete. FPE134 was refurbished to Citylink standards and was based at St Andrews depot.

MSF 751P was a Seddon Pennine VII/Alexander M Type C42Ft purchased new by Eastern Scottish as its XS751 in June 1976. This small batch were the only 12-metre Seddons built, and originally carried Scottish blue livery for use on the London services. They were later demoted and received Citylink livery, and it has to be said they were looking a little bit dated by this time, but they were still very comfortable to travel on. MSF 751P had reached Newcastle and was loading for the return journey home. Sister bus MSF 750P has been preserved and restored to its original livery and looks superb.

K140 RYS was a MAN 11.190/Optare Vecta B37F purchased new by Express Travel of Perth in May 1993. The company passed to British Bus and was merged with Bruce of Airdrie before being closed down. This bus was snapped up by Stevenson's of Uttoxeter, and when that company was taken over by British Bus it was included. Arriva bought out BB and this passed from Arriva Midlands to Arriva North East as its 1558.

G262 UAS was a Volvo B10M-60/Plaxton Paramount 3500 C46Ft purchased new in October 1989 and seen in Glasgow's Renfrew Street as it heads to the bus station. Rapson's had issues working for National Express at this time as vehicles had to be leased rather than purchased outright, in line with Rapson's usual policy. It later passed to Ambassador Travel.

A120 GLS was a Leyland Tiger TRBTL11/2RP/Alexander TC Type C47F purchased new by Midland Scottish as its MPT120 in August 1983. This was the prototype TC Type body and it also carried a non-standard version of Scottish Citylink decals. It is seen leaving Glasgow for a journey to Oban. It would pass to Kelvin Scottish in June 1985 and become 4317 in that fleet, based at Stepps depot. It had become WLT 976 with fleet number 4230 by the time it had joined Kelvin Central Buses in 1989. By 1993 it was with Stagecoach Bluebird and was re-registered yet again to A663 WSU.

N808 NHS was a Volvo B10M-62/Jonckheere C53F purchased new by Park's of Hamilton in February 1996, and used for a time on Scottish Citylink duties. It was leaving Glasgow on service 963 bound for Dundee. It would later become B17 HTL with Heyfordian Coaches of Bicester.

E749 JAY was a Volvo B10M-61/Duple 340 C53Ft purchased new by Henry Crawford of Neilston in March 1988, shown working on the Glasgow to Aberdeen service. It passed to Knightrider of Shotts, and was re-registered as A4 KRT and used on a service competing with Scottish Citylink.

BMS 512Y was a Leyland Tiger TRBTL11/2R/Alexander TE Type C49F delivered new to Midland Scottish as its fleet number MPT112 in April 1983. It originally carried the company's blue and cream livery complete with the famous bluebird emblem, but this was changed to Scottish Citylink colours after just a few months. This was taken around 11.00 p.m. in the coach park at Southwaite Services.

This Leyland Tiger TRCTL11/2RH/Alexander TC Type C47F was new to Fife in 1985 and is seen entering Glasgow's Anderston Cross bus station on service 985, which ran from 6 July 1986, linking Fife and Falkirk to Butlin's holiday camp, Ayr. It was the replacement for service 501, but was itself withdrawn from 7 February 1987. The coach is on the return trip, heading for Leven, and was based at nearby Aberhill depot. On disposal it passed to Shaftsbury & District and was re-registered to YAZ 6394.

M36 KAX was a Volvo B10M-62/Plaxton C49Ft purchased new by Bebb Travel of Llantwit Fardre in March 1995. It was operated by First Edinburgh for a summer season on Scottish Citylink work and this view catches it on the Glasgow to Edinburgh service 900, operating from Linlithgow depot. It later passed to Andrew's of Foxton.

G478 SYS was a Duple 425 SDA1512 C53F delivered new to Bob Chapman, t/a Gold Circle of Airdrie, in May 1990, shown leaving Glasgow on service 904, which will take it to London and Gatwick Airport. It later passed to Shire Coaches of Park Street, Herts.

A51 JLW was a Scania K112CRS/Jonckheere C51Ft purchased new by Derek Randall of London in June 1984, but is shown while owned by Gardiner of Holytown, re-registered as A401 JGU. It was photographed in the Ayrshire coastal resort of Largs while operating a private hire.

E318 OPR was a Volvo B10M-61/Van Hool Alizee C53F purchased new by Excelsior Holidays of Bournemouth in April 1988. It passed to Dodd's of Troon in March 1989 before receiving Scottish Citylink livery seven months later and was reseated to C46Ft the following year. It was repainted into this style of livery in May 1986, and was caught in Hamilton.

FHS 749X was a Volvo B10M-61/Duple Goldliner C53F purchased new by Park's of Hamilton in April 1982, and seen in Inverness bus station with Rapson's Coaches of Alness. Both Scottish Citylink and National Express had been courting Rapson's to sign up as a contractor, but it was the policy of National Express to lease standard types to operators rather than let them choose their own coaches that sealed the deal.

B224 VHW was an MCW Metroliner DR130/3 CH83F new to Wessex of Bristol as its number 224 in July 1984. It passed to Bruce of Airdrie and was painted into Scottish Citylink livery. It was working on service 500 from Glasgow to Edinburgh in this view taken in Buchanan bus station. Bruce of Airdrie was owned by British Bus at this time. On disposal it passed to Ensign for conversion to open-top for use on London sightseeing duties.

F551 TMH was a Volvo B10M-60/Van Hool Alizee C53F purchased new by Travellers of Hounslow in March 1989. It passed to Owen's of Chapellhall and was used on Scottish Citylink work. It was the loss of this work that led to Scottish Highway Express being formed to compete along the busy Glasgow to Edinburgh corridor.

N619 USS was a Volvo B10M-62/Plaxton Premiere C44Ft new as Stagecoach Bluebird number 619 in September 1995. It is shown as number 52310 in Fort William, with the registration plate 703 DYE. It was heading for Edinburgh on service 913.

N805 NHS was a Volvo B10M-62/Jonckheere C53F purchased new by Park's of Hamilton in February 1996, seen leaving Glasgow on service 963, bound for Dundee. This coach would later work for Renown Travel, Mann's Travel of Gravesend and Goldstar Coaches.

This busy scene taken at St Andrew Square bus station in Edinburgh shows three Citylink coaches of different styles, owned by Park's of Hamilton and Rapson's Coaches of Alness. The bus station was opened in April 1957 by the operator Scottish Motor Traction, with sixteen stances over five platforms and underground subways connecting the platforms. By the late 1960s, an office block had been built above the station. Its building supports ate into the platforms and so reduced the available space.

C110 JCS was a Leyland Tiger TRCLXC/2RH/Duple 320 C49Ft delivered new as Central Scottish C10 in April 1986. It would pass to Bluebird Buses in 1989, get re-registered as HSK 760 and be allocated fleet number 455. The Scottish Bus Group companies dropped out of Citylink work one by one, and were replaced by more and more independents.

Scottish Citylink Coaches

CST 390W was a Volvo B58-61/Van Hool Alizee C49Ft purchased new by Rapson's of Brora in May 1981. It ran for a spell as TOI 9785, before passing to the associated Rapson's of Alness fleet. It was re-registered as LIJ 595 and appeared in Scottish Citylink livery. It was resting in Glasgow between duties.

S869 OGB was a Dennis Dart SLF/Alexander ALX200 B40F purchased new by Arriva Scotland West in December 1998. It was allocated to Johnstone depot and given Scottish Citylink livery for use on the Glasgow to Glasgow Airport service. This service could probably trace its roots back to the service by Lowland Motorways-owned Greyhound Coaches, which linked Renfrew Airport to Glasgow St Enoch Square.

M100 WCM was a Dennis Javelin/Plaxton C53F purchased new by Craig of Campbeltown in January 1995 for its West Coast Motors fleet. It was re-registered to M165 HSU before disposal to McColl's Coaches, allowing West Coast to reuse the original plate. It would eventually become NIL 7250 with Frimley's Coaches of Surbiton.

KSK 978 was a Volvo B10M-62/Plaxton Premiere 3500 C53F delivered new to Park's of Hamilton in November 1999. There were ten coaches in this batch, and this one is shown in Princes Street in Edinburgh, as it returns to Glasgow on service 900. This route now runs on fifteen-minute headways for much of the day, with journeys even running through the night.

YJ05 PYP was a VDL SB4000/Van Hool T9 C49Ft purchased new by Craig of Campbeltown for its West Coast Motors fleet in June 2005. It was captured in Glasgow while working on the Scottish Citylink service to Aberdeen. It later gained fleet livery and was re-registered to L100 WCM.

M275 TSB was a Volvo B10M-62/Van Hool Alizee C53Ft purchased new by Crawford's of Neilston in May 1995, shown here working on the Glasgow to Inverness service. It later passed to Long's of Salsburgh and was used on a Motorvator service between Glasgow and Edinburgh that was launched to compete against Citylink. It then moved to Nicoll of Laurencekirk before joining Milligan's of Mauchline as MIL 2978.

E979 LRN was Volvo B10M-61/Duple 340 C49Ft delivered new to Bleanch of Hetton-le-Hole in March 1988. It is seen passing through Hamilton while owned by Bob Chapman of Airdrie, working on the Citylink service to London. It later passed to Bell's of Winterslow and was re-registered as FXI 73.

V906 DPN was a Volvo B10M-62/Jonckheere Mistral C49Ft delivered new to East Kent as its 8906 in September 1999 for use on National Express work. It later became number 52656 with Stagecoach Strathtay, and is shown in Glasgow. Later it was re-registered as YJU 694. It was working on Megabus service M8, bound for Dundee.

SV09 EGY was a Volvo B12B/Plaxton Panther C49FLt purchased new by Stagecoach Highlands in July 2009 as its fleet number 53108. It was caught arriving in Inverness, despite roadworks slowing it down as it crossed the River Ness. It was later transferred to Stagecoach Fife fleet to work in the Rennie's fleet and was re-registered as YJU 656.

R902 JGA was a Volvo B10M-62/Van Hool Alizee C53F purchased new by Park's of Hamilton in January 1998, shown passing through St Andrew Square in Edinburgh. It later worked for Coach Style of Chippenham and Mike De Courcey of Coventry, where it became MJI 7472.

YN14 PNE is a Scania K360EB/Irizar i6 C59Ft delivered new to West Coast in 2014, shown on a private hire to Dumbarton. The Irizar Group is a Spanish-based manufacturer of buses and coaches. Established in 1889, the company is located in Ormaiztegi in the Basque Country. With a commercial presence in over ninety countries, its turnover exceeded 600 million euros in 2017.

RFM 62M was a Daimler Fleetline CRG6LX/Northern Counties H43/29F purchased new by Chester City Transport as its number 62 in December 1973. It was later converted to open-top layout, and is shown working for Bruce of Airdrie Ltd. The original Bruce of Airdrie company had been taken over by Clansman Monarch, which had at one time been the holiday division of Scottish Citylink. The Glasgow coat of arms on the front of RFM 62M had to be removed after objections from the city council and was replaced by a saltire.

YJ55 BJZ was an Optare Solo M850 B22F with extra luggage accommodation for use on Scottish Citylink service 905, which linked Glasgow Airport to the city centre. A major diversion caused the M8 motorway to be closed and the buses had to go via Paisley for a spell. On disposal it passed to Western Greyhound and was re-registered to WK55 BUS.

H856 AHS was a Volvo B10M-60/Plaxton Paramount C53F delivered to Park's of Hamilton in March 1991. It was caught working for Scottish Citylink on the Edinburgh to Glasgow service 500. It would later become A9 TPT with Tayside Greyhound Coaches.

M950 EGE was a Dennis Dart/Plaxton Pointer B40F purchased new by Dodd's of Ayr in December 1994, and passed to Stagecoach Western in June 1997 as fleet number 401. It was given Stagecoach fleet number 32381 in the national series. It was transferred to Stagecoach Glasgow and given Scottish Citylink colours, allegedly for use on the Glasgow Airport service after difficult negotiations with other contractors broke down.

F105 SSE was a Volvo B10M-61/Plaxton Paramount C53F purchased new by Alexander's (North East) of Aberdeen in May 1989. The company was acquired by Grampian Regional Transport and this coach was re-registered as ESK 958. It was then transferred to the associated Midland Bluebird fleet as its number 204, and is shown in Glasgow, working for National Express.

G879 ODS was a Volvo B10M-60/Van Hool Alizee C55F, purchased new by Bruce of Airdrie in August 1989 and shown here in Buchanan bus station in Glasgow. Van Hool introduced the Alizee body in 1978 and produced many in the following years, until it was replaced by the T9 range.

H846 AHS was a Volvo B10M-60/Plaxton Paramount 3500 C53F purchased new by Park's of Hamilton in March 1991. It passed to Bruce of Airdrie and received this livery for Clansman Monarch coach holidays. These tours could be traced back to those operated by Alexander's and SMT. In 1994 businessman Derek Mair bought the firm and expanded it, but it went into liquidation in 2003, leaving debts of £890,000.

HSK 660 was a Volvo B12M/Jonckheere C53F purchased new by Park's of Hamilton in March 2003, shown working on the Glasgow to Aberdeen service. Note the saltires on the mirrors. In 1994 Jonckheere became a part of the Berkhof Group, which was subsequently acquired by VDL Groep in 1998. The official name of Jonckheere was then changed to VDL Jonckheere.

S495 UAK was a Dennis Javelin/Plaxton Premier 320 C10F purchased new by Spring Mobile Training of Goodworth Clatford as a mobile classroom/computer unit in August 1998. It was acquired by Sandy Rapson at an auction in 2003 and fitted out as a fifty-seater with a toilet. The coach was given Scottish Citylink livery and was leaving Glasgow on the long journey to Inverness via Aviemore. It would last to become a sixty-seven seater with Stagecoach Highlands, numbered 59177, when it purchased the company and was latterly re-registered as JAZ 9855.

G542 LWU was a Volvo B10M-60/Plaxton Paramount 3500 C49Ft purchased new by Wallace Arnold Tours (Devon) in March 1990. It joined the Rapson's fleet in 1993 and was re-registered as 4234 NT. This registration number was obtained from an ex-Newton of Dingwall Van Hool coach acquired with the Highland Omnibuses business.

FJ53 VDN was a Dennis R410/Caetano Enigma C49Ft delivered new to Reliant of Heather in February 2004, and used on Grand UK coach holiday work. It was one of a pair acquired by Red Lion of Blantyre for use on Citylink work, and is seen in Princes Street in Edinburgh while working on service 909, bound for Stirling.

You can spot the different front end styling on the Alexander-bodied coaches, parked together in Glasgow Buchanan bus station. Western Dennis Dorchester N220 NCS carried a TC Type body, while Midland Scottish Leyland Tiger BSV807 (A117 GLS) had a TE Type version.

MSC 555X was a Leyland Tiger TRCTL11/3R/Duple Goldliner III C46Ft new as Eastern Scottish XH 555 in July 1982. It came to Midland as its MPT148 in March 1988, having previously been Kelvin Scottish 4327. It would later be rebuilt to Goldliner II spec and be re-registered as SSU861.

Scottish Citylink Coaches

R775 PST was a Volvo B10M-62/Jonckheere Mistral C43Ft purchased new in January 1998. It was loading in St Andrew Square bus station in Edinburgh while working for Scottish Citylink. It would later be re-registered to WXI 878, MIL 5673 and R769 RSS. It was acquired by Stagecoach with the business and became 52675 before transfer to Stagecoach Western. On disposal it passed to McColl's Coaches as its 4002 and gained the registration number MUD 490.

M730 KJU was a Volvo B10M-62/Jonckhere Deauville C49Ft delivered new to Monetgrange, t/a Dunn-Line of Nottingham, in February 1995. It was acquired by Park's of Hamilton and put to work on Scottish Citylink work. It is shown while working on service 500, bound for the Scottish capital.

J633 KGB was a Toyota Coaster HDB30R/Caetano C21F delivered new to Bruce Coaches of Airdrie in April 1992 for use on Clansman Monarch coach tours work, and is seen on Cathedral Street in Glasgow. On disposal it passed to Speedlink Airport Services, based in Crawley. However, it would return to Scotland as Highland Country number 33.

B605 LSO was an MCW Metro-Hiliner HR131/3 C48Ft delivered new as Northern Scottish NCM5 in March 1985, shown arriving at Guild Street bus station in Aberdeen with the destination screen already set for London. The Metro-Hiliner featured a higher floor than the original CR126 model. All were built with the revised frontal styling of the later CR126s. Sales amounted to twenty-one, which were built in 1983–88. The first vehicle was retained by MCW as a demonstrator, while seven were bought by Northern Scottish.

Scottish Citylink Coaches

K924 RGE was a Volvo B10M-60/Jonckheere C53F delivered new to Park's of Hamilton in May 1993. It is seen in Wellington Street in Glasgow, heading for Anderston bus station to pick up passengers before completing its journey to Ayr. It would later be purchased by Midland Bluebird.

A pair of Van Hool Alizee-bodied coaches sit side by side in Glasgow Buchanan bus station. West Coast Motors DAF SB3000 M400 WCM carries the full livery, while the Park's Volvo B10M KSK 978 has Citylink decals applied to its base white. It was common for extra coaches to run like this for the summer season.

J633 KGB was a Toyota Coaster HDB30R/Caetano C21F delivered new to Bruce Coaches of Airdrie in April 1992 for use on Clansman Monarch coach tours work, and is seen working on the short-lived Glasgow city tour. In 1968, Salvador Caetano became the importer for Toyota, introducing the brand in Portugal. Since 2003 it has been assembling the Dyna medium truck for export to several Western European markets.

D144 HMS was a Leyland Tiger TRTL11/3RH/Duple 340 C49Ft purchased new by Midland as its MPT144 in May 1987. It was captured working on Scottish Citylink service 564 as it arrived in Aberdeen. It had just been repainted out of Red Knight livery and was looking very smart.

Scottish Citylink Coaches

TSX 1Y was the prototype MCW Metroliner DR130/1 CH53/16Dt, built as a demonstrator by Metro-Cammell Weymann, Birmingham, in August 1982. It was loaned to the Scottish Bus Group and initially saw service with Western, but was eventually purchased and allocated to Northern, as shown in this night-time shot. It later became a sightseeing bus in London and was re-registered as SNU 122.

L7 TCC was a Volvo B10M-62/Plaxton Premiere C53F purchased new by Travellers of Hounslow in March 1994. It passed to Mairs of Aberdeen and later became FSU 335. It then became K500 KHT with Kingshouse Travel before joining the Essbee fleet in Coatbridge, where it became TNZ 4453.

L110 OSX was a Dennis Javelin 12SDA/Plaxton Premiere C53F new as Eastern Scottish CD10 in May 1994. It passed to SMT, First Edinburgh and First Glasgow, but that was still in the future when it was captured in Falkirk on a crew change over.

A204 FSA was an MCW Metroliner CR126/6 C48Ft new as Northern Scottish NCM4 in December 1984. It was working on the epic journey on route 806 from Plymouth to Aberdeen, which was the longest journey operated at the time. I always thought these coaches seemed to lack power, which was evident when going uphill especially.

H854 AHS was a Volvo B10M-60/Plaxton Paramount 3500 C53F delivered new to Park's of Hamilton in March 1991, just in time for the busy summer season operating for Clansman Monarch coach holidays. It is seen on departure from Glasgow and was on the 'Taste of the Highlands' tour.

C672 KDS was a Volvo B10M-61/Caetano Algarve C49Ft purchased new by Park's of Hamilton in March 1986. It is shown in the ownership of Bruce of Airdrie, after being reliveried for the resurrected Londonliner service, which Citylink reintroduced as a low-cost anti-competition service. It was actually just working on the Glasgow to Edinburgh service as a duplicate, however.

FWT 621Y was a Volvo B10M-61/Plaxton Paramount 3200 C53F new in February 1983 to Wray's of Harrogate. It later served with Ford of Gunnislake before joining Sandy Rapson's fleet. It was photographed leaving Glasgow, heading for Inverness on a Scottish Citylink working, and had been re-registered as UCV 206Y.

C350 DWR was a Scania K112TR/Plaxton Paramount 4000 CH55/20Ft new as National Travel (East) number 350 in April 1986. On disposal it worked for Terminus of London, before it was purchased by Western Scottish in 1988 and allocated fleet number LA110.

Scottish Citylink Coaches

K402 JSR was a Volvo B10M-60/Plaxton Paramount C49Ft new as Strathtay Scottish SV2 in August 1992. It was renumbered as 402 in March 1993, re-registered as VOH 640 in February 1998 and repainted into this livery in May 1999. After disposal it was exported to Zimbabwe.

A124 ESG was a Leyland Tiger TRCTL11/3RH/Duple Caribbean II C47Ft new as Midland Scottish MPT124 in June 1984. It is shown after re-registration to VSU 715, departing Buchanan bus station in Glasgow on service 905, bound for London.

G262 UAS was a Volvo B10M-60/Plaxton Paramount 3500 C46Ft purchased new in October 1989 and seen in Glasgow as it starts its journey to Birmingham. It later passed to Ambassador Travel. The Rapson Group was Scotland's largest independent operator for a while, trading as Rapson's Coaches, Highland Country Buses, Orkney & Causeway Coaches and also operating on long-distance Scottish Citylink/National Express contracts, operating over 250 vehicles with approximately 400 employees.

J510 LRY was a Volvo B10M-60/Caetano Algarve C49Ft delivered new to Bob Chapman, t/a Gold Circle of Airdrie, in January 1992 for the Aberdeen to Gatwick Airport service. It passed to Dunn Line of Nottingham, then Rennies of Dunfermline registered as J15 NLS, and then McDonald of Cumbernauld and Ellenvale Coaches as HIL 5835.

YR17 RHA is a Scania K410EB6/Irizar C59Ft purchased new by Edinburgh Coach Lines in May 2017 for use on Citylink Gold services out of Edinburgh. The firm originated on 16 June 1978 as Silver Fox Coaches of Edinburgh and then Silver Coach Lines Ltd. It was then bought out by the Eirebus Group in Dublin to merge with its Edinburgh-based coach company Edinburgh Castle Coaches and officially changed its name to Edinburgh Coach Lines Ltd in January 2005.

J450 HDS was a Volvo B10M-60/Plaxton Premiere 350 C53F purchased new by Park's of Hamilton in May 1992. There were apparently issues with the build quality of the early Premieres with leaks reported, and also issues with the side panels. Plaxton eventually got to grips with these, but some important customers decided to look elsewhere.

ASA 8Y was a Leyland Tiger TRCTL11/2R/Duple Dominant Express C47F delivered new as Northern Scottish NCT8 in February 1983. It was loading in Nairn bus station on the service linking Inverness to Aberdeen. Note the Scottish Holidays fleet names carried. It would end its days as CSO 389Y with Stagecoach Busways.

F250 OFP was a Dennis Javelin 12SDA/Duple 320 C57F purchased new by Middleton of Rugeley in November 1988. It was acquired by SMT as its XD19, from Martin's of Spean Bridge in 1992, converted to C53Ft and re-registered as A19 SMT. It is shown in Glasgow bus station in Scottish Citylink livery. It passed to the associated Midland Bluebird fleet in 1996.

A156 XFS was a Volvo B10M-61/Van Hool Astral CH48/10Dt purchased new by Rennie's of Dunfermline in May 1984. It was re-registered as MSP 333 for a spell, then became A817 FSF before disposal to Bruce of Airdrie in August 1985. It was re-registered yet again, becoming 2191 RO, and was given Londonliner decals on its Citylink livery.

LSK 495 was a Volvo B10M-62/Van Hool Alizee C53F purchased new by Park's of Hamilton in February 1995. It received route branding for Scottish Citylink service 901, which linked Glasgow to Gourock once an hour. This service was later operated by Cityliner of Greenock, an ancestor of the present McGill's of Greenock.

B924 BGA was a Volvo B10M-53/Plaxton Paramount 4000 CH55/9Ft purchased new by Newton's of Dingwall in April 1985. It passed to the Scottish Bus Group with the business in December 1985, and was allocated to Highland, then Western. It is shown, while owned by Bruce of Airdrie, in Inverness bus station. It was later re-registered as HIL 8437.

KSK 981 is a Volvo B9R/Plaxton Elite C51Ft purchased new by Park's in July 2013 for use on Scottish Citylink service 909, which connects Stirling and Dunblane to the Scottish capital. This service was once part of the Firstbus network.

Scottish Citylink Coaches

YT13 YUD was one of a batch of five Scania K360EB/Irizar i6 C59Ft coaches purchased by Craig of Campbeltown to launch a service linking Glasgow to Edinburgh Airport, branded as CitylinkAir. Early indications, however, pointed to very low loads being carried, but things seemed to have improved over time. This service is operated by the Fairline subsidiary, now renamed as Scotline Coaches.

P927 KYC was a Volvo B12T/Van Hool CH57/14Ct purchased new by Park's of Hamilton subsidiary Trathens Travel Services, based in Plymouth, in March 1997. It was re-registered as DSV 246, then returned to the main Park's fleet in Scotland. It was re-registered as LSK 512 and used on Citylink work. It later served with Stuart's of Carluke and Thandi Coaches as RED 57.

Dodds of Troon WSV 532 was a Volvo B10M with Italian Padane ZX C49Ft coachwork, painted in Scottish Citylink livery. It was new to Trathens Travel Services of Plymouth as its number 42 in June 1982, registered ADV 142Y, but it was acquired by Dodds from Townsend-Thoresen, Tunbridge, in 1986.

SD14 YDG is a Volvo B11R/Jonckheere C53FLt purchased new by Shiel Buses of Acharacle in August 2014 for use on Scottish Citylink duties. It was heading south out of Fort William bound for Glasgow on service 915. Shiel Buses is a local family-owned business based in the Scottish Highlands celebrating over forty successful years in business, providing bus and coach hire services throughout the West Lochaber area in Scotland and beyond.

LSK 509 was a Volvo B12B/Plaxton Panther C49FLt new to Park's of Hamilton in May 2006. It was re-registered to MH06 XNJ just prior to disposal. It passed to D&E Coaches of Inverness in 2011 and became S9 YST. It was repainted into Citylink livery in October 2011, and it is shown in Inverness bus station looking very smart.

C118 DWR was a Volvo B10M-61/Plaxton Paramount C50F purchased new by Wallace Arnold Tours of Leeds in May 1986. It passed to Bruce of Airdrie and was repainted into Scottish Citylink livery, but was photographed before the decals were applied. It was later re-registered to HIL 8439. The company was purchased by British Bus and became Bruce of Airdrie Ltd, but was later closed down by BB, with some vehicles being transferred to Clydeside 2000, including this one, which was numbered as 139.

Seen climbing through Glencoe on a dark day in December, Rapson's Volvo B10M/Plaxton Paragon is heading for Glasgow on service 914. Its journey would have started in Inverness bus station. It is in the second version of Scottish Citylink livery, which was designed by Ray Stenning.

T41 BBW was a MAN 24.350/Jonckheere Monaco CH53/15Ft delivered new as Thames Transit number 41 in July 1999. It was transferred to Stagecoach Glasgow Scottish, and outshopped in Scottish Citylink livery as number 50041. This coach was later sold to Little of Ilkeston before passing via Poppleton of Pontefract to Hunter's of Leeds.

SP62 CHK is a Volvo B13RT/Plaxton Panther C61FLt purchased new in October 2012 as Rennie's 54123. It was leaving Glasgow on a Megabus M8 service to Dundee. In March 2008, it was announced that Stagecoach Fife had bought Rennie's of Dunfermline for an undisclosed sum. The fleet had sixty vehicles and included eighteen double-deckers, which were all leased from Stagecoach. They were formally based at Dunfermline (Wellwood Mill) before moving to Cowdenbeath in 2016.

448 GWL was a Volvo B10M-61/Jonckheere CH49/9Ft purchased new by Titterington's of Blencow in July 1983, and passed to Rapson's in 1985. It is seen resting in Glasgow's Buchanan bus station. The cherished registration plates would be reallocated to newer vehicles as time went by.

FJ56 OCB was a Scania K340EB4/Caetano Levante C49FLt purchased new by Thames Transit as its fleet number 59214 in February 2007. It was acquired by West Coast Motors in 2014 and is now re-registered as J80 WCM. The Caetano Levante was adopted as the standard type for National Express.

B224 VHW was an MCW Metroliner DR130/3 CH83F new to Wessex of Bristol as its number 224 in July 1984. It passed to Bruce of Airdrie and was painted into Scottish Citylink livery. It was working on service 500 from Edinburgh to Gourock in this view taken in Glasgow. Bruce of Airdrie was owned by British Bus at this time. On disposal it passed to Ensign for conversion to open-top for use on London sightseeing duties.

N138 YMS was a Scania K113CRB/Van Hool C53F new to Clydeside in April 1996. It was one of a batch of four allocated to Greenock depot and used on the Gourock–Glasgow–Edinburgh service. The staff on Citylink work were on a lower pay scale than service bus drivers. After a while it was decided to opt out of such work because there was very little return on the investment required and a deal was brokered with Park's of Hamilton for them to take on the service and the vehicles. Although they were decidedly non-standard for Park's, it operated them for a little while.

C660 KDS was a Volvo B10M-61/Caetano Algarve C49Dt purchased new by Park's of Hamilton in March 1986. It is shown in a damp Dunfermline, working for Bruce of Airdrie, with Londonliner decals. It was only in 1967 that the first Caetano coaches were imported in the UK. A strategic alliance between Mitsui & Co., Ltd and CaetanoBus was signed. Caetano electric chassis were officially presented at Coach & Bus UK 2017.

H619 UWR was a Volvo B10M-60/Plaxton Paramount C50F delivered new to Wallace Arnold Tours of Leeds in March 1991. It passed to Rapson's and was given the cherished plate from an ex-Newton's of Dingwall Volvo. It was working on Citylink service and is seen at Scrabster. The ferry terminal is located on the north coast of Scotland, 1.5 miles from Thurso, 22.5 miles from Wick and 112 miles from Inverness.

V312 NGD was a Dennis Dart SLF/Plaxton Pointer B39F delivered new as Arriva Scotland West number 799 in December 1999. It is shown arriving at Buchanan bus station in Glasgow, with the destination screen already set for the return journey to Glasgow Airport. Arriva would later sell its Scottish operations to McGill's of Greenock.

A117 GLS was a Leyland Tiger TRBTL11/2RP/Alexander TE Type C47F new as Midland Scottish MPT 117 in August 1983. It was transferred to Kelvin Scottish as its fleet number 4322 in June 1985 and re-registered as WLT415, which was changed to A253 WYS to allow its disposal to Midland Scottish in 1988. It would later become BSV 807 for a spell before returning to A253 WYS prior to sale to Linco Travel in Dorset, later passing to Frontera Travel.

N139 YMS was a Scania K113CRB/Van Hool Alizee C53F new as Clydeside Buses number 139 in April 1996. It passed to Park's of Hamilton, then Lodge of High Easter before reaching Flagfinders of Braintree, where it was re-registered as XIL 8427. The Scania 3-series bus range was introduced in 1988, with the K93 and K113 the most common chassis for coaches, which had a longitudinally rear-mounted engine.

C349 LVV was a Volvo B10M-61/Caetano Algarve C57F purchased new by Newton's of Dingwall in September 1985. Three months later it passed to the Scottish Bus Group with the business and was allocated to the Central Scottish fleet as its C9. It passed to the merged Kelvin Central Buses fleet in 1989 and on disposal went to Marbill of Beith.

BDV 863Y was a Volvo B10M-61/Berkhof C49Ft purchased new by Trathen's of Roborough as its number 63 in March 1983. Rapson's purchased it from Sowerby of Gilsland as XUJ 427Y before re-registering it as ESK 985. This is quite a rare shot of it running as XUJ 427Y with Rapson's. There was a much greater variety of types used in the early days of Citylink, utilising various contractors to fulfil its needs.

YY14 NLN was a Volvo B9R/Plaxton Elite C49Ft purchased new by Lochs of Leurbost in July 2014, but is now with Shiel Buses. It is shown in Fort William shortly after acquisition and had yet to receive any Citylink lettering. The fleet now runs in excess of forty-five vehicles, ranging in size from sixteen-seater luxury mini coaches to forty-nine-seater luxury coaches and double-deckers.

G950 VBC was a DAF SB2300/Caetano C53F purchased new by Bob Chapman, t/a Gold Circle of Airdrie, in August 1989. The Chapman family are still involved in the coach industry with Silverdale Coaches and are still based at Flowerhill Industrial Estate, former home of the Gold Circle business.

Park's of Hamilton SF57 XEP was a Volvo B12B/Plaxton Panther C48FL, which carried Citylink decals and was captured in Princes Street in Edinburgh. It would later become Y30 HMC with Hallmarks Coaches, which was part of Rotala North West.

HSK 649 is a Volvo B13R/Plaxton Elite C46FLt purchased new by Park's of Hamilton in March 2015 for use on Citylink Gold duties. The first use of the 'Citylink Gold' brand was introduced on 5 June 2017 for services between Edinburgh and Inverness. Two Citylink Gold journeys in each direction were introduced seven days a week.

E218 GNV was a Volvo B10M-61/Jonckheere C51Ft new to The Londoners in September 1987. It was acquired by Silver Fox of Renfrew and used on Scottish Citylink duties. It passed to John Morrow of Clydebank in 1993, where it became 216 TYC, and has also served with Hills of Stibb Cross and Alpha of Honiton. It has carried quite a few other registrations including E754 NWP, B6 GBD and FIG 6431.

F760 ENE was a Volvo B10M-61/Van Hool Alizee C49Ft purchased new by Smith-Shearings as its number 760 in January 1989. On disposal it passed to Park's of Hamilton and was re-registered as GIL 1682. It was given Citylink colours, and was caught in Glasgow. It later passed to Ramsay of Elsrickle for further service.

R264 OFJ was a Volvo B12T/Van Hool Astrobel CH57/14Ct purchased new by Trathens Travel Services, Plymouth, in February 1989. It passed to the main Park's of Hamilton fleet and was given Scottish Citylink livery. It was captured as it departed from Glasgow's Buchanan bus station.

YX63 NGE is a Volvo B13R/Plaxton Panther C61FLt purchased new by Western as fleet number 54131 in September 2013. It was working for Scottish Citylink on the Glasgow to Edinburgh service. In these vehicles the rearmost axle is connected to the steering, with the rearmost set steering in the opposite direction to the front axle. This steering arrangement makes it possible for the longer tri-axle coaches to negotiate corners with greater ease than would otherwise be the case.

SF10 GXL was a Bova Futura FHD127.365 C53FLt purchased new by Stuart's of Carluke in April 2010. It was captured in Glasgow working on Megabus service M8 bound for Dundee. The Bova Futura coach is usually fitted with a DAF engine, which was first introduced in the 1980s and continues in production as of 2018 as the VDL Futura.

B175/6 FFS were a pair of Volvo Citybus B10M-50/Alexander RVC Type CH42/28Fs purchased new by Fife Scottish as FRA75/6 in October 1984. They were transferred to Western in 1987, primarily for use on Scottish Citylink service 501, which linked Edinburgh to Ayr via Glasgow. In a very rare moment the pair were captured together in Glasgow.

N48 MJO was a Volvo B10M-62/Berkhof C51Ft purchased new by Thames Transit as its number 48 in April 1996 for the Oxford Tube. It passed to Stagecoach for Citylink work in Scotland, and Stagecoach Fife number 520 is seen here at Cowdenbeath depot looking very smart. It would become 52038 and see further service with Bluebird before sale to Castell of Caerphilly, where it became N48 MJO once again.

R264 OFJ was a Volvo B12T/Van Hool Astrobel CH57/14Ct purchased new by Trathens Travel Services, Plymouth, in February 1989. It passed to the main Park's of Hamilton fleet and was given Scottish Citylink livery. It was captured as it departs from Glasgow's Buchanan bus station.

Scottish Citylink Coaches

F986 HGE was a Volvo B10M-60/Plaxton Paramount C53F delivered new to Park's of Hamilton in March 1989. It passed to Clyde Coast Coaches in March 1990 before purchase by Mair's of Aberdeen for Citylink work, and is shown in Glasgow. It later became PSU 626 and was allocated fleet number 732.

T52 BBW was a MAN 24.350/Jonckheere Monaco CH53/15Ft purchased new by Thames Transit as its number 52 for use on Oxford Tube services. On disposal it passed to Western and is caught as it leaves Glasgow while working on the Edinburgh Express for Scottish Citylink. It would later work for Mitcham Belle.

NCS 125W was a Volvo B10M-61/Duple Dominant III C46Ft purchased new by Western Scottish as its V125 in June 1981. It passed to Clydeside Scottish as its P425 in June 1985. On disposal it passed to Midland-Bluebird as number 201 before joining Whitelaw's of Stonehouse. It was caught in Peterborough in July 1986.

B332 LSA was a Leyland Tiger TRCTL11/2RP/Alexander TC Type C47Ft new as Northern Scottish NCT32 in January 1985. It was re-registered as TSV722 for a spell and passed to Stagecoach with the business. It later worked for MacEwan's of Dumfries, and was reunited with its old registration plate.

Scottish Citylink Coaches

P720 RWU was a DAF SB3000/Van Hool Alizee C49Ft new to London Coaches (Kent) in August 1996. It joined the West Coast fleet in 2005 and is seen leaving Oban for Fort William on service 918. Craig of Campbeltown has been a contractor for Citylink for many years now, although relations have broken down once or twice.

SD14 YDH was a Volvo B11R/Jonckheere C53FLt purchased new by Shiel Buses of Acharacle in August 2014, which has subsequently gained full Citylink livery. It has been re-registered as K800 SBL, and was working on the Glasgow to Skye service.

N866 XMO was a Dennis Javelin 12SDA/Berkhof Excellence 1000 C53F purchased new by Q-Drive, Battersea, in May 1996. It was three years old when it joined Rapson's in 1999, and was given decals for the Inverness to Skye service. It was re-registered to IDZ 828 in 2003.

BSG 547W was a Leyland Tiger TRCTL11/3R/Duple Dominant III C46Ft new as Eastern Scottish XH547 in July 1981. It passed to Kelvin Scottish and has been registered as WLT 742 and WGB 176W. It was transferred to Northern Scottish in 1989 and rebuilt to Dominant IV spec as C51F. It passed to Stagecoach with the business as its number 434.

Stagecoach Western Volvo B12B/Plaxton Panther 54068 in a white livery, with Citylink lettering, is shown operating service 900 to Edinburgh. It had been new to Stagecoach Bluebird in October 2009. The Plaxton Panther body has been built by Plaxton in Scarborough, North Yorkshire, since 1999, and is still in production.

CSG 783S was a Seddon Pennine VII/Plaxton Supreme Express C45F purchased new by Eastern Scottish in February 1978. It briefly ran for Midland Scottish in early 1985, when it assumed control of the routes run from the former Baillieston garage. The vehicles were all transferred to Stepps and passed to Kelvin Scottish in June 1985. This coach had been reseated to Citylink spec and would become S10X with Kelvin. It would have a very short life, however, and went for scrap in 1987.

This Clydeside Scottish Dennis Dorchester/Plaxton Paramount 3500 C55F was on a tour of the Highlands and Islands. It had just returned from Mull and was heading up the west coast to reach its next port of call at Fort William. It became policy to remove individual company fleet names from the coaches.

Rapson's 162 EKH was a Volvo B10M-61/Jonckheere Jubilee CH47/10Ft, originally B22 FJS, while sister 448 GWL was purchased second hand from Titterington's of Blencow. The location was Highland Omnibuses' Inverness depot after Rapson's had acquired the business. Rapson's was founded in 1945 but came to the fore in the 1970s and 1980s. In August 1991, Highland Scottish was sold to a consortium made up of Rapson's Coaches and Scottish Citylink for £800,000. In March 1993, ownership of Highland Scottish passed wholly to Rapson's.

Scottish Citylink Coaches

L44 SAS was one of a pair of Scania K93s with Plaxton Premiere 320 coachwork, operated by Travel Dundee on the Scottish Citylink network for a few years. As its number plate might suggest, they were transferred from Speedlink Air Services in London. The location was St Andrew Square bus station in Edinburgh.

D144 HMS was a Leyland Tiger TRTL11/3RH/Duple 340 C49Ft purchased new by Midland Scottish as its MPT144 in May 1987. It was captured working on the low-cost Scottish Citylink Red Knight-branded route linking London and Inverness, introduced to combat competition on the corridor.

F105 SSE was a Volvo B10M-61/Plaxton Paramount C53F purchased new by Alexander's (North East) of Aberdeen in May 1989. The company was acquired by Grampian Regional Transport and the coach was re-registered as ESK 958. It was then transferred to the associated Midland Bluebird fleet as its number 204, and is shown in Glasgow as 2204.

VSS 4X was a Leyland Tiger TRCTL11/3R/Duple Goldliner III C46Ft new as Northern Scottish NLT4 in July 1982. It was transferred to Strathtay Scottish in June 1985, and is seen in a nonstandard version of Citylink livery as it heads through Stirling. It was re-registered as WLT 921 in 1987, then MSL 185X. It was rebodied by East Lancs in April 1992.

Scottish Citylink Coaches

YX63 NGF is a Volvo B13R/Plaxton Panther C61FLt purchased new by Stagecoach Western as its 54132 in September 2013. Behind is Park's of Hamilton KSK 877, which was also working on the 900 Edinburgh–Glasgow service.

S464 JGB was a Volvo B10M-62/Plaxton Premiere C53F purchased new by School Bus Scotland, Port Glasgow, in August 1998. This firm was part of the Argyll Group, and a forerunner of McGill's of Greenock. Citylink later withdrew from the Glasgow to Gourock corridor, leaving the field free for McGill's.

N805 NHS was a Volvo B10M-62/Jonckheere C53F purchased new by Park's of Hamilton in February 1996. It is seen in Edinburgh bus station, outside the Travel Centre, where passengers could purchase tickets and get information. The coach later worked for Manns Travel of Gravesend, Renown Travel and Goldstar Coaches.

A504 PST was a Leyland Tiger TRCTL11/3R/Duple Laser C46Ft new as Highland Scottish E2 in February 1984. It was transferred to Midland Scottish in June 1985, and later re-registered as 889 MHX. It is seen in Glasgow, screened up for a journey to Ayr on service 501. The original Laser was introduced in 1983 and the design featured gasket glazing, which distinguished it from the high-floor Duple Caribbean body.

KSK 981 is a Volvo B11RT/Plaxton Elite C57FLt purchased new by Park's of Hamilton in May 2016, seen arriving at Glasgow Buchanan bus station on the 900 service from Edinburgh. The Elite body was unveiled at the Euro Bus Expo at the National Exhibition Centre, Birmingham, in November 2008 by the British manufacturer Plaxton. It went into production in late 2008. The vehicles are easily identifiable due to the Boeing 747-like curved roof at the front end. Elites on scheduled express routes have a low-level destination board, resulting in a larger front window than most comparable coaches.

B187 CGA was a Volvo B10M-61/Berkhof Emperor CH48/12Ft purchased new by Western Scottish as its V187 in February 1985. It was supplied by Ensign (dealer). On disposal it passed to Marbill of Beith and Irvine's of Law as B550 EGG.

P20 GRT was a Scania L94IB/Irizar C51Ft delivered new to Grampian as number 714 for its Mair's of Aberdeen subsidiary in June 1997. It is shown leaving Glasgow, heading back to Aberdeen on service 965. It had operated for First Edinburgh, Eastern Counties, Midland Bluebird, Western National and Hants & Dorset before arriving in Glasgow in 2006. Sold in January 2009, it moved to Abbott's of Leeming, then Walters, Oxfordshire.

M731 KJU was a Volvo B10M-62/Jonckheere Deauville C49Ft purchased new by Monetgrange, t/a Dunn-Line of Nottingham, in February 1995. It was acquired by Park's of Hamilton and put to work on Scottish Citylink work. It is shown while working on service 900, bound for Gourock. It passed to Paul's Coaches of Stoke-on-Trent, then Ayrways of Ayr as K700 AYR.

A173 UGB was a Leyland Tiger TRCLXC/2RH/Plaxton Paramount Express 3200 C49F new as Western Scottish L173 in April 1984. It passed to Clydeside Scottish in June 1985 and had a long life, later becoming 407 CLT, a registration taken from a London Routemaster. It is shown at Kilmarnock depot.

N286 OYE was a Volvo B10M-62/Plaxton Premiere C53F delivered new to Pullmanor, t/a Redwing Coaches of Camberwell, in March 1996. It passed to Alex Kean for his Cityliner Express operations, and is seen in Greenock working on service 901. Alex owned many companies in the bus industry, the last being a share in McGill's of Greenock and First Stop Travel.

B132 PMS was a Leyland Tiger TRCTL11/3RH/Duple Laser 2 C46Ft purchased new by Midland Scottish as its MPT132 in April 1985, and was on display for the launch of all the new Scottish Bus Group companies. It would later become SSU 837. The Laser was built by Duple between 1983 and 1986. It replaced the long-running Duple Dominant body as Duple's standard medium-height coach of the mid-1980s.

E183 KNH was a DAF MB230DKFL/Caetano Algarve C49Ft purchased new by Prentice of West Calder in May 1988, shown in Elder Street in Edinburgh carrying the cherished registration number 570 PRR. Prentice has over seventy years of trading experience, and is one of the largest and longest established family-run coach hire companies in Scotland. It was originally based in West Calder and, most recently, Edinburgh, through the acquisition of Edinburgh Group Travel.

Scottish Citylink Coaches

G454 TST was a Volvo B10M-60/Van Hool Alizee C55F delivered new to Clan Garage of Kyle, t/a Skyeways, in August 1989. It is shown leaving Glasgow to head north to Fort William. Relations later broke down between Scottish Citylink and Skyeways, and they went into competition with each other, with Citylink eventually winning the fight.

M45 KAX was a Volvo B10M-62/Plaxton Premiere Expressliner C46Ft new to Bebb of Llantwit Fardre in March 1995. It was purchased by Rapson's in 1998 and later carried the registration plates 9637 EL and HDZ 5407. It was resting between duties at the Rapson's depot in Seafield Road in Inverness.

B229 LSO was a Volvo B10M-61/Van Hool Alizee C49Ft purchased new by Mair's of Bucksburn in January 1984. The company was purchased by the privatised Grampian Regional Transport and retained as a stand-alone business for a spell before being moved into the King Street depot in Aberdeen, home of the main fleet.

G450 DSB was a Volvo B10M-60/Duple 340 C55F purchased new by Craig of Campbeltown in April 1990, shown arriving in Glasgow on service 926 from Campbeltown. The firm is better known as West Coast Motors, and was founded in 1921. It is a major contractor for Citylink, and was even part-owned by Citylink at one time, although it is fully owned by the Craig family once again.

Scottish Citylink Coaches

KSK 982 is a Volvo B11RT/Plaxton Elite C61Ft purchased new by Park's of Hamilton in April 2017, seen in Perth while working on Megabus service M8 bound for Dundee. Most of the network is nowadays operated by tri-axle coaches. Park's provides vehicles for both Citylink and its own City to City Coaches and these are a common sight throughout Scotland.

V73 DSN was a Volvo B10M-62/Plaxton Premiere 350 C48Ft delivered new as Tayside Coaches TC23 in October 1999. It was captured leaving Glasgow on service 963, going back to its home town. It would later pass to the associated Wishart's of Friockheim fleet.

C112 DWR was a Volvo B10M-61/Plaxton Paramount 3500 C50F purchased new by Wallace Arnold tours, Leeds, in April 1986. It was acquired by Rapson's Coaches and given Scottish Citylink livery. It was later re-registered as ESK 932, as shown in this view taken in Hamilton. It was heading for London via Milton Keynes and Coventry.

YX67 UPJ is a Volvo B11R/Plaxton Elite C49FLt new as Stagecoach Highlands 54821 in October 2017. It was loading in Fort William for Inverness. Stagecoach in the Highlands is the division of the Stagecoach Group that covers most of the former Rapson Group bus and coach operations following the takeover by Stagecoach in May 2008.

YS16 LML is a Scania K410EB6/Irizar C53Ft purchased new by Craig of Campbeltown in July 2016, seen in Glasgow. This service is operated by coaches based at the Charles Street depot in Glasgow, acquired with the Fairline Coaches business, which has now been rebranded as Scotline Coaches.

L55 SAS was a Scania K93CRB/Plaxton Premiere 320 C47Ft purchased new by Speedlink Airport Services as its fleet number S55 in September 1993. It passed to Travel Dundee in 1998 and was initially used on Scottish Citylink work, but later became part of the Tayside Greyhound coach fleet as EUE 489.

F912 YNV was a Volvo B10M-61/Jonckheere Deauville C51Ft delivered new to Eurocoach of Northampton in March 1989. It passed to Grampian Regional Transport as its number 91 and was re-registered as TSU 682 in July 1991 before transfer to the associated Midland Bluebird fleet as number 203 in 1992. It was seen passing through Dundee.

KSK 977 was a Volvo B10M-62/Plaxton Premiere 350 C53F delivered new to Park's of Hamilton in November 1999. It was re-registered as V94 LYS for disposal, and later joined Prentice Westwood as WNB 604 and GHZ 8752. It was passing through St Andrew Square in Edinburgh while working on the Glasgow to Edinburgh route.

E318 OPR was a Volvo B10M-61/Van Hool Alizee C53F purchased new by Excelsior Holidays of Bournemouth in April 1988. It passed to Dodd's of Troon in March 1989 before receiving Scottish Citylink livery seven months later and was reseated to C46Ft the following year. It was working on service 276, bound for Hull via Newcastle.

A502 FRS was an MCW Metroliner DR130/4 CH69DT purchased new by Northern Scottish as its NDM2 in July 1984, shown after arriving at London Victoria coach station. It would be cleaned and refuelled for the return journey later that day. It passed to Western Scottish as its LM158 in 1989, and later to Mactavish's Coaches of Dalmuir.

BDV 863Y was a Volvo B10M-61/Berkhof C49Ft purchased new by Trathen's of Roborough as its number 63 in March 1983. Rapson's purchased it from Sowerby of Gilsland as XUJ 427Y before re-registering it as ESK 985. It was leaving Wick to return to Inverness.

A165 TGE was a Leyland Tiger TRCTL11/3RZ/Duple Caribbean C46Ft new as Western Scottish L165 in June 1984 and originally delivered in London livery. The year 1989 saw it transferred to Northern, becoming its NCT43 and carrying Scottish Citylink livery. It was working on the Glasgow to Aberdeen service.

KSK 977 was a Volvo B13RT/Plaxton Panther C61FLt purchased new by Park's of Hamilton in July 2013, captured in Stirling while working on the 909 service bound for Edinburgh. It had recently been repainted into the new City to City livery used by Park's on the joint network marketed by Scottish Citylink.

YN15 EKD was a Scania K360EB4/Irizar C51FLt purchased new by West Coast Motors in April 2015 for the Glasgow to Skye route, but has since been displaced by new vehicles. It was caught on a private hire for the Kintyre Pipe Band in Dumbarton.

WWA 47Y was a Volvo B10M-61/Van Hool Alizee C46Ft purchased new by Trevor Carnell of Sheffield in June 1983. It passed to Rapson's and was re-registered as 9637 EL, as shown in this view taken in Glasgow. It was working on service 955 from Inverness.

B569 LSC was a Leyland Tiger TRCTL11/3RH/Duple Caribbean C46Ft new as Eastern Scottish XCL 569 in April 1985. It was captured in Glasgow while working on Scottish Citylink service 501, bound for Edinburgh. At the end of 1984 the Caribbean range was given a facelift and renamed the Caribbean II. The main difference was a revised front with twin headlamps and plastic grille.

G845 GNV was a Volvo B10M-60/Jonckheere Deauville C51Ft purchased new by Green's of Kirkintilloch in September 1989 for use on a Glasgow to Edinburgh route in competition with Citylink. It then passed to Marbill of Beith before joining Mair's of Aberdeen and was loading in Edinburgh. It later became 507 EXA with Shropshire Bus & Coach.

TSD 153Y was a Dennis Dorchester SDA801/Plaxton Paramount Express C49F purchased new in March 1983, and is shown in Ayr. It carried a hybrid livery for Highland Express, which was a short-lived budget airline flying between Prestwick and New York, and Scottish Citylink Coaches.

The Duple Dominant III was designed to satisfy a Scottish Bus Group requirement for express coaches, and featured shallow, parallelogram-shaped flat double-glazed side windows. The small windows were designed for SBG's overnight Scotland to London services, where quietness was more important than views. Many SBG Dominant IIIs were rebuilt later in life with larger Dominant I/II or Dominant IV windows to make them more suitable for general coaching work.

E183 KNH was a DAF MB230DKFL/Caetano Algarve C49Ft purchased new by Prentice of West Calder in May 1988 and is shown on a private hire in Glasgow, carrying the cherished registration number RPP 734, before the Citylink lettering was applied.

Scottish Citylink Coaches

Citylink introduced the Red Knight brand as a low-cost travel provider between Inverness and London after competition was unleashed on the corridor. Three coaches were provided by Midland Scottish and all were from the same batch. KSU 834 had started life as D143 HMS and was a Leyland Tiger.

BU18 YOH is a very smart new Mercedes Tourismo Base delivered to Shiel Buses in May 2018 and is seen arriving in Fort William on the Scottish Citylink service to Glasgow. The Mercedes-Benz Tourismo (formerly designated as the Mercedes-Benz O 350) is an integral coach manufactured by Mercedes-Benz since 1994. It was initially manufactured in Hosdere, Turkey. In 2006 a revised version was launched. By 2014, 21,000 had been sold.

TFS 321Y was a Leyland Tiger TRCTL11/2R/Plaxton Paramount 3200 Express C49F new to Eastern Scottish in April 1983 as YL 321. It was transferred to Midland on the closure of Baillieston depot and then passed to Kelvin Scottish in June 1985 with Midland's Glasgow operations. It passed to the merged Kelvin Central in 1989, becoming 4314.

SF13 FMJ was a Van Hool Astromega TDX29 CH38/17Ft new as Stagecoach Western 50305 in July 2013. It was originally a sleeper coach, but is now used on Citylink Gold duties, and was seen in Glasgow. As can be seen throughout the book, standards have continued to rise to meet passenger expectations.